For

. . . .

From

. . . .

Copyright © 2009
Hallmark Licensing, Inc.

Published by Hallmark Books,
a division of Hallmark Cards, Inc.,
Kansas City, MO 64141
Visit us on the Web at
www.Hallmark.com.

Editor: Megan Langford
Art Director: Kevin Swanson
Designer: Mary Eakin
Production Artist: Dan Horton
Photo Research: Jessica Benton

ISBN: 978-1-59530-240-3
BOK4362
Printed and bound in China

GIFT BOOKS
from Hallmark

Friends
for
Life

The
happiest
business
in all the world is that

of making friends.

ANNE S. EATON

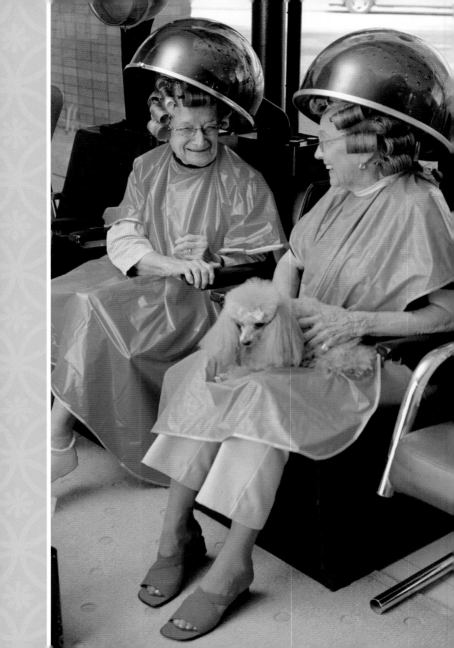

Do you remember the day we first met?
That day, I thought you were:

_____

_____

_____

_____

❋

Three words that best describe
you now are:

1) . . . .

2) . . . .

3) . . . .

I love how when I say
"Remember the time . . ."
it doesn't matter what I say next.
You always remember.

**A story about us that
I never get tired of telling is:**

Friendship needs no words.

DAG HAMMARSKJÖLD

Nothing
can come between
true friends.

EURIPIDES

It's impossible to overestimate
the value of one good friend.
To me, you are:

- ■ generous
- ■ fun
- ■ caring
- ■ independent
- ■ beautiful
- ■ considerate
- ■ sweet
- ■ brave
- ■ funny
- ■ creative
- ■ thoughtful
- ■ sincere
- ■ kind

- ■ ....
- ■ ....

Here are some quirky things
I love about you:

_____

_____

_____

_____

_____

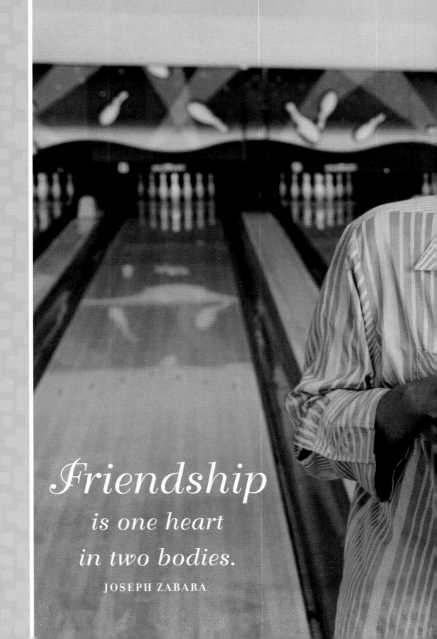

Friendship
is one heart
in two bodies.

JOSEPH ZABARA

FRIEND ('frend) *n* : someone who
knows you're fibbing if you say
"Everything's fine," when it's really not.

Thanks for being there for me
through some tough times.
I especially appreciate the time you:

_____

_____

_____

_____

_____

The
greatest
gift of life
is friendship.

HUBERT HORATIO HUMPHREY

I love it when you:

- call me to chat about nothing

- hug me

- sing along to the radio

- let me cry on your shoulder

- laugh at my jokes

- act silly

- keep my secrets

- wave at me across a crowded room

- water my plants when I go out of town

- . . . .

- . . . .

The friend who holds your hand
and says the wrong thing
is made of *dearer stuff*
than the one who stays away.

BARBARA KINGSOLVER

*No man is the whole of himself;
his friends are the*
rest of him.

HARRY EMERSON FOSDICK

Thank you for inspiring me to:

_____

_____

_____

_____

_____

✳

Without your support, I never would have:

_____

_____

_____

_____

_____

A friend hears the
song in my heart
and sings it to me when my

memory fails.

The song that best describes our friendship is:

- ■ **"Wind Beneath My Wings"**
  BY BETTE MIDLER

- ■ **"Thank You for Being a Friend"**
  BY ANDREW GOLD

- ■ **"You've Got a Friend"**
  BY JAMES TAYLOR

- ■ **"That's What Friends Are For"**
  BY DIONNE WARWICK AND FRIENDS

- ■ **"Lean on Me"**
  BY BILL WITHERS

One of my favorite things is recognizing your name in my in-box among the sea of spam.

Some of my other favorite things about you are:

_____

_____

_____

_____

_____

*A friend is a person
with whom I may be
sincere.*

RALPH WALDO EMERSON

I've always wanted to tell you:

_____

_____

_____

_____

_____

If we were in a movie together,
it would be:

- ■ a slapstick comedy
- ■ a serious drama
- ■ an action-adventure film
- ■ a melodramatic musical

This is who would star as you:

. . . .

This is who would star as me:

. . . .

Life is good when you're among good people. And you, my friend, are good people.

The thing I admire most about you is:

. . . .

. . . .

But every road is
rough to me
that has **no friend**
to cheer it.

ELIZABETH SHANE

The beauty of nature and
the company of friends
are always welcome.

**Some of my favorite things
to do with you are:**

_____

_____

_____

_____

_____

Spending time with you is:

- ■ fun
- ■ wonderful
- ■ memorable

- ■ . . . .
- ■ . . . .

We could just sit on the porch
and watch the world go by,
and as long as you're there,
I'd savor every minute of it.

A friend is a
present
you give yourself.

ROBERT LOUIS STEVENSON

You've given me some incredible gifts.
One of my favorites was:

_____

_____

_____

Old jeans, old sneakers,
old friends—the good stuff just gets
better with time.

Here are some ways
you've changed my life:

_____

_____

_____

_____

_____

It's the ones you can
call up at 4:00 A.M.
that *really*
matter.

MARLENE DIETRICH

**How many hours do you think
we've spent talking on the phone?**

- ■ 10
- ■ 100
- ■ 1000
- ■ too many to count

A friend is someone
who makes me feel
totally
acceptable.

ENE RIISNA

"Stay" is a charming word in a friend's vocabulary.

*The growth of friendship
may be a* lifelong affair.

SARAH ORNE JEWETT

If you were wine, you'd be:

- ■ White Zinfandel (sweet)
- ■ Cabernet Sauvignon (rich and full-bodied)
- ■ Chardonnay (dry, yet beloved by all)
- ■ Chianti (best when aged)

I love
everything
that's old:
old friends, old times,
old manners, old books,
old wines.

OLIVER GOLDSMITH

Thank you for teaching me how to:

_____

_____

_____

_____

_____

❁

Without you, I may never have:

_____

_____

_____

_____

_____

Friends are born,
not made.

HENRY BROOKS ADAMS

A good friend is the
purest *of all God's gifts,*
for it is a love that has
no exchange of payment.

FRANCES FARMER

I hope that when we're both old and gray,
you'll look back on our friendship and say:

_____

_____

_____

_____

_____

-▫-

If I wrote a book about us,
the title would be:

_____

_____

True happiness consists not in the multitude of friends, but in the worth *and* choice.

BEN JOHNSON

Happiness
seems made to be
shared.

JEAN RACINE

Thanks for sharing your:

- handbag
- jewelry
- scarf
- hairdresser's phone number

- ....
- ....

A friend is one who
knows you
and loves you

just the same.

ELBERT HUBBARD

How beautiful it is,
the face of a friend.

To me, you are:
- ■ lovely
- ■ beautiful
- ■ gorgeous
- ■ all of the above

*We have such a friendship
that is given to
very few.*

BETTE DAVIS

**Here are a few reasons I'm lucky
to have you as a friend:**

_____

_____

_____

_____

_____

✖

With friends, "making cookies"
doesn't have to involve actually
baking the cookie dough.

If you were a cookie, you'd be:

- chocolate chip
  (everybody loves it)

- gingersnap (a little sassy)

- peanut butter (always classic)

- triple chocolate chunk
  (can't get enough of it)

- . . . .

*We cherish our friends
not for their ability to amuse us,
but for ours to*
amuse them.

EVELYN WAUGH

You always make me laugh when you:

_____

_____

_____

_____

_____

Good friends
are good for
your *health.*

DR. IRWIN SARASON

You keep me young when you:

_____

_____

_____

_____

_____

Friends are full of
all kinds of sweetness.

The older

the friend the better.

PLAUTUS

I predict that in ten years, we'll be:

_____

_____

_____

_____

_____

✳

And we find at the end of
a perfect day
the soul of a friend we've made.

CARRIE JACOBS BOND

If you have enjoyed this book
or it has touched your life in some way,
we would love to hear from you.

Please send your comments to:
Hallmark Book Feedback
P.O. Box 419034
Mail Drop 215
Kansas City, MO 64141

Or e-mail us at:
booknotes@hallmark.com